For the Teacher

This reproducible study guide to use in conjunction with a specific novel consists of lessons for guided reading. Written in chapter-by-chapter format, the guide contains a synopsis, pre-reading activities, vocabulary and comprehension exercises, as well as extension activities to be used as follow-up to the novel.

In a homogeneous classroom, whole class instruction with one title is appropriate. In a heterogeneous classroom, reading groups should be formed: each group works on a different novel on its reading level. Depending upon the length of time devoted to reading in the classroom, each novel, with its guide and accompanying lessons, may be completed in three to six weeks.

Begin using NOVEL-TIES for reading development by distributing the novel and a folder to each child. Distribute duplicated pages of the study guide for students to place in their folders. After examining the cover and glancing through the book, students can participate in several pre-reading activities. Vocabulary questions should be considered prior to reading a chapter; all other work should be done after the chapter has been read. Comprehension questions can be answered orally or in writing. The classroom teacher should determine the amount of work to be assigned, always keeping in mind that readers must be nurtured and that the ultimate goal is encouraging students' love of reading.

The benefits of using NOVEL-TIES are numerous. Students read good literature in the original, rather than in abridged or edited form. The good reading habits, formed by practice in focusing on interpretive comprehension and literary techniques, will be transferred to the books students read independently. Passive readers become active, avid readers.

Novel-Ties® are printed on recycled paper.

SYNOPSIS

Eleven-year-old April Hall wants to be in Hollywood with her glamorous mother, actress Dorothea Dawn. Sent to live with a grandmother she barely knows, April predicts that she will not like her new life in a shabby university town. She doesn't expect to be accepted or to make friends. Her perspective changes as she gets caught up in the Egypt Game.

A voracious reader with a wild imagination, April shares her interest in Egypt and "all sorts of ancient stuff" with her new neighbor Melanie Ross. The two girls spend the month of August together, much of the time playing imaginary games of their own invention and reading whatever they can find about Egypt. In the beginning of September, they discover the perfect place to play Egypt—a deserted storage yard behind a dingy curio shop.

Together with Melanie's young brother Marshall, the two girls clean up the storage yard and set up altars to the good queen/goddess Nefertiti and to the evil god Set. While adjusting to school, April and Melanie, with Marshall in tow, continue to play Egypt, composing and practicing rites and ceremonies in the afternoons and on weekends. They eventually include Elizabeth Chung, a new neighbor with a decided resemblance to Nefertiti. Of the four, only Marshall has an inkling that they are being watched by the Professor, the reclusive owner of the curio shop.

The murder of a neighborhood child brings a temporary halt to the Egypt Game. Forbidden to play outdoors, the children design elaborate Egyptian costumes and plan for their return. On Halloween night, they slip away from a chaperoned Trick-or-Treat group to answer the summons of "the Mighty Ones." Toby and Ken, two sixth-grade boys, noisily interrupt the return ceremony. Desperate to keep their game a secret, the girls invite the boys to join them.

The original Egyptians are amazed at Toby and Ken's willingness to play the game. Toby comes to the next meeting and suggests that they finish an alphabet of hieroglyphics to write secret messages. Ken comes laden with new ornaments, including a stuffed owl to represent Thoth, the bird-headed god of wisdom and writing. An elaborate burial ceremony for Elizabeth's pet parakeet ushers in a good week in the land of Egypt. An equally elaborate ceremony for Consulting the Oracle of Thoth ushers in a scary week.

Both Melanie and Ken are ready to quit the game when the oracle miraculously supplies answers to written inquiries. Even Toby, admitted author of the first two answers, is frightened when Marshall receives an answer to his question. Only after April is attacked in the storage yard and saved by Marshall and the Professor do the Egyptians learn of the Professor's role as secret observer and helpful oracle.

The attack on April marks the end of both the Egypt Game and the Professor's seclusion. At a Christmas party, he explains how watching the Egypt Game has restored his interest in life. He gives keys to the storage yard to the Egypt Game members. April and Melanie contemplate playing a new game in which they will be playing gypsies.

BACKGROUND INFORMATION

Ancient Egypt

Egypt's 5,000-year-old civilization was once the greatest in the world. Along a fertile strip on both sides of the Nile, dynasties of Kings and Queens lived and prospered, leaving a monumental legacy that continues to fascinate people today. Without machinery, the Egyptians built tombs and temples, monoliths and pyramids that still stand. Early on, they developed a system of writing called hieroglyphics and kept written records. Lovers of beauty, they created great works of art and literature. The first culture to emphasize life after death, the Egyptians buried their treasures to take with them for a comfortable afterlife. Preserved in the dry Egyptian sand, many of these treasures have been excavated. Along with written records, they provide a firsthand look at life in ancient Egypt.

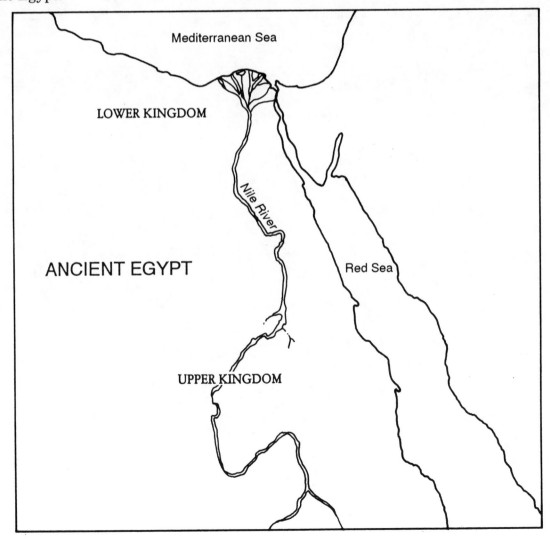

PRE-READING ACTIVITIES AND DISCUSSION QUESTIONS

1. Preview the book by reading the title and author's name and by looking at the illustration on the cover. What do you think the book will be about? Do you think it will take place in present or past time? Have you read any other books by the same author?

2. **Cooperative Learning Activity:** Read the Background Information on page two of this study guide and do some additional research to fill in the first two columns of a **K-W-L** chart, such as the one below. Complete column three after you finish the book.

Ancient Egypt		
– K – What I Know	**– W –** What I Want To Know	**– L –** What I Learned

3. *The Egypt Game* takes place the summer that eleven-year-old April Hall begins a new life in a new neighborhood. How do you think she might feel about being the "new kid on the block"? How do you feel about meeting people? How do you feel about having new experiences?

4. April tries to make a strong impression on the people she meets. Do you think first impressions are important? Do you think that they are accurate? How do you act when you are trying to make an impression on someone?

5. April's new neighbor Melanie Ross hopes April will become a real friend. What is a real friend? What qualities do you look for in a friend? Is it important that he or she be like you? Why or why not?

6. Do some research to learn about hieroglyphics, the pictographic script of the ancient Egyptians. Find illustrations of hieroglyphics that have been found at ancient sites. What do the hieroglyphs reveal about courtly life and life among commoners in ancient Egypt.

7. Do you believe in the possibility of supernatural events? Have you ever read about any, or have you had any experiences that suggested a supernatural cause? Take an informal poll of your classmates to find out who believes in extraterrestial beings, the ability of some people to foretell the future or read the thoughts of others, and the possibility of summoning spirits from the past.

THE DISCOVERY OF EGYPT, ENTER APRIL,
ENTER MELANIE—AND MARSHALL

Vocabulary: Use the context to help you select the best meaning for the underlined word in each of the following sentences. Circle the letter of the answer you choose.

1. The store had a <u>dingy</u> appearance because it had not been swept for months and the windows were coated with dirt.

   a. insignificant   b. bright   c. shabby   d. rowboat

2. Wisps of hair escaped from the girl's <u>straggly</u> ponytail.

   a. straight   b. neat   c. messy   d. late

3. It was obvious that the <u>residents</u> of the apartment house took pride in their home because they picked up litter outside every day.

   a. physicians   b. dwellers   c. officials   d. owners

4. While digging in the desert, the <u>archeologist</u> discovered a tomb filled with gold.

   a. person who designs buildings   b. person who studies ancient objects   c. person who shoots with a bow and arrow   d. angel of high rank

5. When I have spare time, drawing is my favorite <u>occupation</u>.

   a. possession   b. talent   c. event   d. activity

6. The <u>haughty</u> waiter smirked at us when we asked for a description of an item on the menu.

   a. too proud   b. popular   c. too humble   d. foolish

> Read to find out about April's new friendship when she comes to live with her grandmother for the summer.

Questions:

1. Why do the children in the neighborhood avoid the Professor, and why do few local residents shop in his store?

2. How is "The Discovery of Egypt" both a play on words and an appropriate title for the first chapter?

3. Who are the children who cleared the Professor's storage yard to play the Egypt Game? What is their relationship to one another?

4. Why is April at the Casa Rosada? How does she feel about being there?

The Discovery of Egypt, Enter April, Enter Melanie—and Marshall (cont.)

5. How is April's reaction to the Professor different from that of all the other children?

6. What impression does April want to make on Melanie? Does she succeed?

7. Why does April stop acting "grown-up and Hollywoodish"?

Questions for Discussion:

1. Why do you think April has trouble expressing feelings of pleasure or affection? How do you know she likes Melanie?

2. Do you think April's grandmother is happy to be taking care of April? Does she seem to love April? What kind of a relationship do you think might develop between them?

Literary Device: Flashback

A flashback is an interruption in a story to tell about events that happened at an earlier time. At the beginning of *The Egypt Game*, the Professor watches three neighborhood children playing in the storage yard behind his store.

What important information about these children is provided by the flashback in the next two chapters?

_____

_____

_____

What background information is still missing?

_____

_____

Why do you suppose the author begins the book with the chapter "The Discovery of Egypt" rather than "Enter April"?

_____

_____

_____

The Discovery of Egypt, Enter April, Enter Melanie—and Marshall (cont.)

Literary Elements:

I. *Mood*—Mood is the overall atmosphere or feeling of a story. Happiness or sadness, excitement or boredom—mood can be any strong feeling or emotion the author creates, often by using descriptive details. What feeling does Zilpha Keatley Snyder create with her descriptions of the A-Z store and the Professor in "The Discovery of Egypt"?

_____

_____

What specific words or phrases help set the mood?

_____

_____

II. *Characterization*—Use the Venn diagram below to compare April and Melanie. Write the qualities that the girls have in common in the overlapping part of the circles.

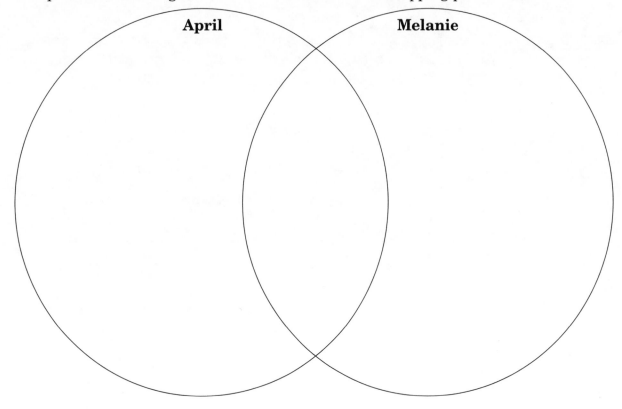

Writing Activity:

Write about an actual or an imagined time when you made a new friend. Tell about your first impressions of each other and why you became friends. Indicate how the two of you are alike and how you are different.

THE EGYPT GIRLS, THE EVIL GOD AND THE SECRET SPY

Vocabulary: Draw a line from each word on the left to its definition on the right. Then use the numbered words to fill in the blanks in the sentences below.

1. authority
2. drastic
3. elaborate
4. relieved
5. sacred
6. scouted

a. hunted around to find something
b. extreme or severe
c. dedicated to religious purpose
d. accepted source of expert information
e. freed from fear or anxiety
f. worked out with great care

. . . .

1. We made _____ plans so that nothing would go wrong the night of the party.

2. The advertising agency chose a leading _____ on tooth decay to recommend the toothpaste.

3. After worrying all night, I am _____ to hear that you arrived safely.

4. Some ancient peoples built _____ fires to worship their gods.

5. She _____ around for her keys for hours, but still could not find them.

6. When the prisoners would not listen to reason, the police took _____ measures to end the riot.

Read to find out whether April makes a good first impression at her new school.

Questions:

1. What do April and Melanie both worry about at the beginning of school? How are Melanie's worries different from April's?

2. Why does finding the bust of Nefertiti seem like a magical omen to April and Melanie?

3. How does the character of Set start? What makes him seem to be more than a character in a game?

4. Who is the secret spy referred to in the chapter title "The Evil God and the Secret Spy"?

The Egypt Girls, The Evil God and the Secret Spy (cont.)

Questions for Discussion:

1. How would you describe April's attitude and behavior toward her grandmother? Why do you think April feels and acts the way she does? Do you think April is being fair?

2. Why do you think April plans to wear her false eyelashes to school?

3. April remarks that Marshall is "pretty sharp for a four-year-old." What do you think?

4. Why do you think the children are being spied upon?

Literary Device: Foreshadowing

Foreshadowing refers to the hints or clues an author provides to suggest what will happen later in a story. What might the last sentence in the final paragraph in the chapter called "The Evil God and the Secret Spy" foreshadow?

_____

_____

What feeling or mood does the sentence help create?

_____

_____

Art Connection:

Reread the description of the "Temple" at the beginning of "The Evil God and the Secret Spy." Draw a picture of the setting for the Egypt Game, or put together a cut-paper collage of pictures of ancient Egypt that you find in magazines or sketches from books.

Writing Activity:

How would you stop April from wearing false eyelashes to school? Pretend you are Melanie and write a brief diary entry in which you reveal your own "drastic plan."

EYELASHES AND CEREMONY, NEFERBETH, PRISONERS OF FEAR

Vocabulary: Synonyms are words with similar meanings. Draw a line from each word in column A to its synonym in column B. Then use the words in column A to fill in the blanks in the sentences below.

A		B	
1.	exasperated	a.	ceremonies
2.	maintained	b.	lasting
3.	persistent	c.	compartment
4.	resemblance	d.	annoyed
5.	rites	e.	claimed
6.	vault	f.	likeness

. . . .

1. The man with a square jaw bears a certain _____ to his pet boxer.

2. The woman _____ that she was innocent despite the evidence of her guilt.

3. Every culture has its own burial _____, or procedures for putting the dead to rest.

4. The teacher was _____ by the student's frequent tardiness.

5. I have a(n) _____ cough and sniffle for all the weeks that ragweed is in bloom.

6. The hollow in the tree makes a perfect _____ for hidden treasures.

> Read to find out why the children stop playing the Egypt Game for a while.

Questions:

1. How does Melanie solve the problem of April wearing false eyelashes to school?
2. Why doesn't Melanie worry when April is nicknamed "February" by her classmates?
3. Why do April and Melanie keep sacred records in "Egypt"?
4. Why does April have mixed feelings about becoming Elizabeth's friend?
5. How does Elizabeth come to be known as Neferbeth?
6. What neighborhod event turns the residents into "prisoners of fear"? What is the effect of this event on the Egypt Game?
7. Why does suspicion fall on the Professor? Why don't the three girls believe the professor is guilty?

Eyelashes and Ceremony, Neferbeth, Prisoners of Fear (cont.)

Questions for Discussion:

1. Do you agree or disagree with April's statement, "I guess everybody has something they're not very grown-up about"? What is it that April is not grown-up about?

2. If you were a resident of the Casa Rosada, would you have signed Mr. Schmitt's petition asking the Professor to leave the neighborhood?

3. Do you think that Dorothea is the caring mother that April believes her to be? Do you think she will soon return for April?

Literary Device: Personification

Personification is a device in which an author grants lifelike qualities to nonhuman objects or ideas. Notice how fear is personified, or brought to life, in the following passage:

> As the days passed and no arrests were made, fear and suspicion grew and spread in all directions; and a great silence began to settle over Orchard Avenue and the streets and alleys on either side . . . . But although fear made a great silence out-of-doors, inside the homes and stores and apartments it had a different sound—it talked and it talked and it talked.

What lifelike qualities are given to fear?

_____

What picture does the passage create in your mind?

_____

Art Connection:

Notice how the "Temple" has been improved in the chapter called "Eyelashes and Ceremony." Add to the picture or collage that you began after you read the preceding chapters to reflect these improvements.

Writing Activities:

1. Imagine that Mr. Schmitt has called a neighborhood meeting as part of his campaign against the Professor. Defend your point of view as a resident of the Casa Rosada. Write a speech in which you denounce the Professor or speak up on his behalf. Be prepared to deliver your speech to neighbors.

2. Write about a person you know who, like April, appears one way to strangers and another way to those who know him or her well. Describe these two contrasting appearances and tell why you think this person behaves in such a way in public.

SUMMONED BY THE MIGHTY ONES, THE RETURN TO EGYPT, EGYPT INVADED

Vocabulary: Choose a word from the Word Box to replace each underlined word with a more exact word that clarifies the meaning of the sentence. Write the word on the line at the right of the sentence.

```
                    WORD BOX
     chaperoned       omen       summoned
     demonstration    quavered   teetering
```

1. The tenants organized a <u>parade</u> to protest the rent hike. _____

2. On school trips we are <u>accompanied</u> by at least one parent. _____

3. The video showed Humpty Dumpty <u>swaying</u> and about to fall. _____

4. The disorderly students were <u>called</u> to the principal's office. _____

5. Breaking a mirror is often considered a bad <u>sign</u>. _____

6. The young boy's voice <u>shook</u> as he described the car accident. _____

Read to find out if the children return to their hideout.

Questions:

1. How does the Egypt gang manage to get back to Egypt? What are the dangers they face in doing this?

2. How does April inform Elizabeth that they are going to Egypt on Halloween night? Why does Melanie go along with April's scheme if she thinks it is "downright disobedient" and "deadly dangerous"?

3. How does the Egypt gang decide upon the moment to return to their hideout? According to Melanie, what do the gods require of the gang upon their return to Egypt? Why?

4. How does the gang respond to the gods' demand?

5. What puts an end to the gang's ceremony?

Summoned by the Mighty Ones, The Return to Egypt, Egypt Invaded (cont.)

Questions for Discussion:

1. When April first discusses her plans, she notes the difference between not having permission to do something and being "downright disobedient." Do you think there is a real difference?

2. Ken and Toby are described as "just about the most disgusting boys in the sixth grade, in a fascinating sort of way." How do you think April and Melanie really feel about the boys? Are the boys ordinary or are they special?

Literary Element: Humor

Humor in a story is the quality that sometimes makes you laugh aloud and sometimes simply makes you smile as you read. Marshall's down-to-earth comments provide much of the humor in *The Egypt Game*. While the other Egyptians are deadly serious, he lightens the mood. In "Summoned by the Mighty Ones," what comment does Marshall make about the summons that makes the other Egyptians' dramatic chanting seem a little ridiculous?

_____

Describe one other situation where Marshall's actions or comments made you smile or laugh.

_____

Literary Device: Cliffhanger

A cliffhanger in literature is a device borrowed from early, serialized films in which an episode ends at a moment of suspense. In a book a cliffhanger is usually found at the end of a chapter to encourage the reader to continue on in the book.

What is the cliffhanger at the end of the chapter called "Egypt Invaded"?

_____

What do you think is about to happen?

_____

Writing Activity:

Has the Eqypt Game turned "deadly dangerous"? Make a prediction about what will happen next. Then step in for a turn as author and write a paragraph or two to continue the story. Continue reading to see how your version of the story compares with that of the author.

ELIZABETHAN DIPLOMACY, MOODS AND MAYBES, HIEROGLYPHICS, THE CEREMONY FOR THE DEAD

Vocabulary: Use the words from the Word Box and the clues below to solve the crossword puzzle.

WORD BOX
bier
clenched
contemplated
cringed
deciphered
faltered
fluent
mugged
procession
rendezvous
warily

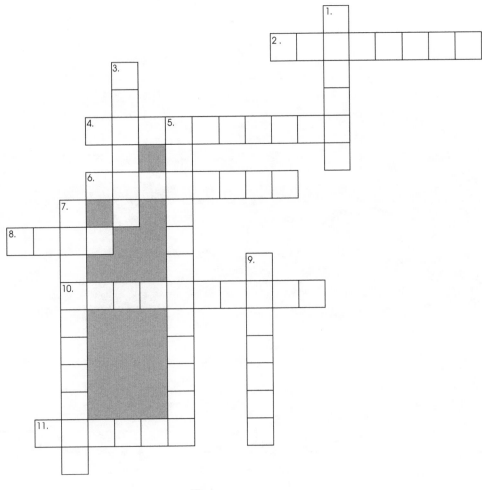

Across

2. hesitated

4. group moving in an orderly line

6. closed tightly

8. stand on which a coffin is placed

10. translated into ordinary language; decoded

11. made a face to get an amused reaction

Down

1. speaking or writing smoothly

3. cautiously; carefully

5. thought about

7. meeting by agreement

9. pulled back, as in fear

Read to find out what April's mother wrote in her letter.

Elizabethan Diplomacy, Moods and Maybes, Hieroglyphics, The Ceremony for the Dead (cont.)

Questions:

1. What is the Elizabethan diplomacy referred to in the chapter title?

2. Why is April in a bad mood after receiving a letter from her mother? How does April's relationship with her grandmother seem to change at this time?

3. How would you describe the first meeting of the enlarged Egypt gang?

4. Why does April object to Toby's suggestion that they finish the alphabet of hieroglyphyics? Why does she change her mind?

5. Why do Ken and Toby tell their friends that they have an after-school job? What does this indicate about their commitment to the Egypt Game?

6. What makes the Ceremony for the Dead particularly important to the Egypt gang?

7. How is Toby's behavior in "Egypt" different from his behavior in school?

Questions for Discussion:

1. Why do you think the boys agree to join the game?

2. Why do you think Toby's behavior with the Egypt gang is better than his behavior at school?

3. Would you want to participate in the Egypt Game? Would you respond to the activities and ceremonies in a manner that is more like Toby or more like Ken?

Literary Device: Metaphor

A metaphor is a suggested comparison. An extended metaphor is one that continues. In "Hieroglyphics" what are the several ways in which the Egypt Game is compared to historical events?

_____

_____

_____

_____

_____

_____

_____

Elizabethan Diplomacy, Moods and Maybes, Hieroglyphics, The Ceremony for the Dead (cont.)

Prediction:

Who do you think is observing the players of the Egypt Game? What do you think will happen now that someone is aware of what the five children are doing?

_____

_____

_____

_____

Writing Activity:

Recall how the Egypt Game has helped April overcome her sadness over the separation from her mother and how it has helped Elizabeth cope with the death of her parakeet. Write about an activity that helped you put aside your own feelings of sadness or anger. Describe the cause of your feelings and tell why you think this activity helped you get through a difficult time.

THE ORACLE OF THOTH, THE ORACLE SPEAKS, WHERE IS SECURITY?

Vocabulary: Use the context to help you select the best meaning for the underlined word in each of the following sentences. Circle the letter of the answer you choose.

1. The king consulted an <u>oracle</u> before invading the neighboring country.

   a. agent of the gods   b. owl   c. encyclopedia   d. world atlas

2. The tour guide <u>hustled</u> the group out of the building and back to the bus that was waiting in the parking lot.

   a. followed   b. hurried   c. led   d. delayed

3. In the quiet of her room, she thought about what had happened and she <u>meditated</u> on the meaning of life.

   a. heard about   b. asked about   c. spoke about   d. thought about

4. With her <u>regal</u> bearing and her rich robes, the imposter was easily mistaken for the queen.

   a. calm   b. royal   c. false   d. military

5. In the director's absence, an assistant <u>presided</u> at the board meeting.

   a. voted upon   b. was dismissed   c. took charge   d. was summoned

6. His hands shook and his voice was <u>wavery</u>.

   a. steady   b. unsteady   c. loud   d. soft

> Read to find out if the children are contacted by a supernatural being.

Questions:

1. Why does the Egypt gang prefer Toby's way of consulting the oracle to April's version?

2. What is disturbing about the oracle's answer to Ken's question?

3. Why are the children startled by the sound of thunder outside the land of Egypt?

4. At what point do the Egyptians first consider quitting the game?

5. Why does Marshall refuse to quit?

The Oracle of Thoth, The Oracle Speaks, Where is Security? (cont.)

Questions for Discussion:

What explanation can you give for the oracle's answers to Ken's and April's questions? Do you think that it is possible that the children have stirred up a supernatural power?

Literary Element: Mood

Sometimes the physical atmosphere, or weather, helps set the emotional atmosphere of a story. Notice how the weather contributes to the mood in the following passage:

> There wasn't much light in the land of Egypt that afternoon, which didn't make it all less strange. The days had been getting shorter, of course, but it was something more than a gradual seasonal change, too. As Toby bowed and mumbled and chanted before the altar of Thoth, his high-priest face looking distant and unfamilar in the deep shadow and flickering candlelight, low black clouds were moving in swiftly from the bay. In the temple it was suddenly so dark that the reflected candles lit Thoth's glassy stare with points of fire.

What mood is set by the passage?

_____

_____

Circle the specific words or phrases that help set the mood.

Writing Activity:

Look back at the oracle's response either to Ken's question or to April's question. What does the mysterious oracle's answer mean? Write a paragraph in which you explain one of the responses. In your paragraph, tell whether or not you think the oracle's response is wise.

CONFESSION AND CONFUSION, FEAR STRIKES, THE HERO

Vocabulary: Select a word from the Word Box to replace the underlined word or phrase in each of the following sentences. Write the word you choose on the line below the sentence.

```
                        WORD BOX
        alibi         incredulous      tension
        conscience    rasped           theories
```

1. Maintaining his innocence, the accused man said, "My <u>inner voice</u> is clear."

   _____

2. We were <u>skeptical</u>; her flying-saucer story was hightly doubtful.

   _____

3. To learn how the fire started, the reporter asked the fire chief about his <u>ideas based on observation and reasoning</u>.

   _____

4. A sore throat left her hoarse. When she tried to speak above a whisper, her voice <u>made a harsh, grating sound</u>.

   _____

5. The detective questioned the suspect about her whereabouts on the night of the robbery; he did not believe her <u>proof of being elsewhere</u>.

   _____

6. He felt his head begin to pound from the <u>mental or emotional stress</u> of being overworked.

   _____

> Read to find out how the Professor rescues April.

Questions:

1. What is Toby's confesson to Arpil and Melanie? Why does he confess?

2. How do the three plan to handle Marshall's questions to the oracle? What spoils their plans?

3. Why do April and Marshall return to Egypt at night?

Confession and Confusion, Fear Strikes, The Hero (cont.)

4. How do the Professor and Marshall save April from her attacker?

5. How does the incident of the attack change the lives of April, Marshall, and the Professor?

Questions for Discussion:

Reread the scene where Caroline comes to the police station after April is attacked. Why do you think this scene is important to the story? How is it different from the last scene in which April cried in her grandmother's presence?

Literary Element: Plot

The plot of a novel refers to its sequence of events. The climax, or turning point, is the most exciting moment in a story. All the action before the climax leads up to it. What event do you think is the climax of *The Egypt Game*?

_____

_____

Does anything in the story still need to be explained?

_____

_____

Writing Activity:

In a journal entry, respond freely to this observation made in "Fear Strikes":

> Imagination is a great thing in long dull hours, but it's a real curse in the dark.

Use the quotation as either a story starter or the moral of a story that you write.

GAINS AND LOSSES, CHRISTMAS KEYS

Vocabulary: Analogies are equations in which the first pair of words has the same relationship as the second pair of words. For example: PRIVATE is to PUBLIC as GAIN is to LOSS. The words in both pairs are antonyms, or opposites. Choose the best word from the Word Box to complete each analogy below.

```
                        WORD BOX
          benefited      lair        intriguing
          conceived      reactions
```

1. AUDITORIUM is to PUBLIC as _____ is to PRIVATE.

2. HARMED is to INJURED as _____ is to GAINED.

3. CAUSE is to EFFECT as ACTIONS is to _____.

4. INNOCENT is to GUILTY as _____ is to BORING.

5. SPECULATED is to THOUGHT as _____ is to PLANNED.

> Read to find out whether April returns home or stays at Casa Rosada.

Questions:

1. Why does business improve for the Professor?

2. Why does April refuse the invitation she receives from her mother?

3. According to the Professor, what had led him to cut off contact with other people?

4. Why had the Professor decided to play oracle?

5. What is the Professor's gift to the children? What is their gift to him?

Questions for Discussion:

1. Do you think April made the right choice in refusing her mother's invitation?

2. What does the Professor mean when he describes his life after his wife's death: "As the years went by, the store and I became dusty junkyards, and after a while I didn't care"?

3. What do you think April's life at the Casa Rosada will be like from now on? What do you think the Professor's life will be like?

Gains and Losses, Christmas Keys (cont.)

Literary Element: Characterization

In many stories, an important event will cause the main characters to change in some important way. In this story, the Egypt Game brings important changes to both April and the Professor. How has each character changed? Record your impressions in the chart below by filling in words to describe April and the Professor at the beginning and the end of the book. In forming your impressions, consider the character's appearance, behavior, thoughts, and actions as well as reactions of others to the character.

	Beginning of Story	**End of Story**
April		
Professor		

Writing Activity:

Write about a real or an imaginary place that would be as special to you as the land of Egypt was to the children in this story. Describe the place and tell how it would remain private. Also, indicate whether you would allow anyone else to join you there.

CLOZE ACTIVITY

The following excerpt has been taken from the chapter entitled "The Egypt Girls." Read it through completely and then go back and fill in the blank spaces with words that makes sense. When you have finished, you may compare your language with that of the author.

April was the most exciting friend Melanie had ever had. No one else knew about so many _____ [1] things, or could think up such marvelous _____ [2] to do. With April, a walk to the _____ [3] could become an exploration of a forbidden _____, [4] or a shiny pebble on the sidewalk could _____ [5] a magic token from an invisible power. _____ [6] April got that imagining gleam in her _____ [7] there was no telling what was going to _____ [8] next. Just about any interesting subject you could _____, [9] April was sure to know a lot of _____ [10] and wonderful facts about it. And if she _____, [11] you could always count on her to _____ [12] up a few, just to keep things _____. [13]

There was only one thing that April didn't _____ [14] to know much about — that was getting _____ [15] with people. Most people, anyhow. With Melanie, April _____ [16] herself, new and different from anyone, wild and _____ [17] and terribly brave. But with other people _____ [18] was often quite different. With other kids she _____ [19] put on her Hollywood act, terribly grown-up and _____ [20] with everything. And with most grown-ups April's _____ [21] got narrow and you couldn't believe a _____ [22] she said.

Melanie had gone to Wilson School _____ [23] her life, and she knew what it _____ [24] like. There were all different kinds of _____ [25] at Wilson; kids who looked and talked and _____ [26] all sorts of ways. Wilson was used to _____. [27] But there were some things that Wilson kids just wouldn't stand for, and Melanie was afraid that April's Hollywood act was one of them.

POST-READING ACTIVITIES AND QUESTIONS FOR DISCUSSION

1. Return to the K-W-L chart on Egypt that you began on page three of this study guide. Fill in the third column with any information you learned while reading the book. Has the book raised any additional questions about ancient Egypt that you would like to research? Compare your chart with those of your classmates.

2. **Cooperative Learning Activity:** What if this story took place in your neighborhood in the present rather than in a university town during the 1960s? What if you and your classmates were the friends whom April met? How would the Egypt Game be different? Work in a small group to write a story plan for a revised version of *The Egypt Game* in which you change the setting, the characters, or both. Your plan should include a brief description of the new setting and/or characters and a brief summary of the changes in the plot.

3. Follow Toby's lead and play oracle. Together with classmates generate a list of questions about the future that you would like answered. Take turns using Bartlett's *Familiar Quotations* or another collection as a source of quotations to provide answers. The quotations you choose may be humorous, sensible, or mysterious.

4. Imagine that seven years have passed since the discovery of Egypt. As April packs her bags for college, she finds her key to the storage yard, thinks back to the summer she moved to the Casa Rosada, and calls her best friend Melanie to talk about it. What would she and Melanie have to say? Take the part of April or Melanie, and together with a friend, dramatize their conversation. Talk about what the Egypt Game meant to you.

5. Imagine that the movie version of *The Egypt Game* is coming soon to a theater near you. Study the movie advertisements in your local newspaper, and design an ad for the movie. In your ad, you might feature the part or parts of the story that you find most exciting. You also might include several quotations from rave reviews.

6. **Social Studies Connection:** Help transform your classroom into Egypt. Use what you have learned about Egyptian culture to decorate the room and to create costumes for an Egypt festival. Then choose a name, a hieroglyphic symbol, and "play Egypt." You might re-enact a ceremony in which the Egypt gang participated. Then make up a ceremony of your own, or design and play a trivia game about Egypt.

7. Find another project for the Egypt gang. Brainstorm a list of possibilities. Then choose a subject of interest and investigate it. Write a persuasive speech in which you present your ideas to fellow Egyptians. Be prepared to deliver this speech to your classmates.

Post-Reading Activities and Questions for Discussion (cont.)

8. **Literature Circle:** Have a literature circle discussion in which you tell your personal reactions to *The Egypt Game*. Here are some questions and sentence starters to help your literature circle begin a discussion.

   - How are you like April? How are you different? Are you like any of the other characters in the story?
   - Do you find the characters realistic? Why or why not?
   - Which character did you like the most? The least?
   - Who else would you like to have read this novel? Why?
   - What questions would you like to ask the author about this novel?
   - I would have liked to see . . .
   - I didn't understand . . .
   - I enjoyed . . .
   - April learned that . . .
   - Melanie learned that . . .

9. **Readers Theater:** Choose one chapter from the book with a lot of dialogue spoken by several characters, such as the chapter entitled "Elizabethan Diplomacy." Assign students to read the roles of each character and one student to read the narration. The characters should read only those words inside the quotation marks, ignoring phrases such as "he said" or "she said." You may want to use some simple props to identify characters and setting.

SUGGESTIONS FOR FURTHER READING

* Burnett, Frances Hodgson. *The Secret Garden*. Random House.
* Byars, Betsy. *The Summer of the Swans*. Penguin.

  Cleaver, Vera, and Bill Cleaver. *Ellen Grae*. HarperCollins.

  Climo, Shirley. *The Egyptian Cinderella*. HarperCollins.

  Conford, Ellen. *Anything for a Friend*. Random House.

  Greene, Constance. *A Girl Called Al*. Penguin.
* Hamilton, Virginia. *M.C. Higgins, the Great*. Simon & Schuster.
* Konigsburg, E.L. *Jennifer, Hecate, Macbeth, William McKinley and Me, Elizabeth*. Random House.
* _____. *From the Mixed-Up Files of Mrs. Basil E. Frankweiler*. Random House.
* Lewis, C.S. *The Lion, The Witch, and The Wardrobe*. HarperCollins.

  McGraw, Elois. *Mara, Daughter of the Nile*. Penguin.
* Paterson, Katherine. *Bridge of Terabithia*. HarperCollins.

  Rylant, Cynthia. *A Blue-Eyed Daisy*. Random House.

  Stolz, Mary. *Cat in the Mirror*. Random House.

  Yep, Laurence. *Child of the Owl*. HarperCollins.

Other Books by Zilpha Keatley Snyder

Black and Blue Magic. Random House.

Blair's Nightmare. Random House.

The Changeling. Random House.

Eyes in the Fishbowl. Random House.

The Famous Stanley Kidnapping Case. Random House.

The Gypsy Game. Random House.

The Headless Cupid. Random House.

Janie's Private Eyes. Random House.

Libby on Wednesday. Random House.

Season of Ponies. Random House.

The Truth About Stone Hollow. Random House.

The Velvet Room. Random House.

The Witches of Worm. Random House.

* NOVEL-TIES Study Guides are available for these titles.

ANSWER KEY

The Discovery of Egypt, Enter April, Enter Melanie — and Marshall

Vocabulary: 1. c 2. c 3. b 4. b 5. d 6. a

Questions: 1. The Professor, who is the owner of the dingy A-Z shop, has such a shabby appearance, bent posture, and stony stare that children and adults keep away. 2. The title in an ordinary context might refer to explorers discovering a new land. Instead, in the context of this book, it refers to the Professor discovering children playing a game of ancient Egypt in his yard. 3. April Hall and Melanie and Marshall Ross cleared the storage yard; April and Melanie are eleven-year-old girls who are new neighbors and friends; Marshall is Melanie's younger brother. 4. April is at the Casa Rosada because she has recently moved in with her grandmother while her mother, who is an actress, is on tour. She is unhappy about being there because she misses her mother and resents her grandmother. 5. April is not afraid of the Professor. In fact, she admires his dead-pan expressions. 6. April wants to appear sophisticated and indifferent to the opinions of others. At first, Melanie thinks that April is sophisticated, but she soon realizes that April is putting on an act. Melanie sees through April's indifference. 7. When she sees Melanie's library, April stops acting "grown-up and Hollywoodish." She gets caught up in the books and forgets her pretense.

The Egypt Girls, The Evil God and The Secret Spy

Vocabulary: 1. d 2. b 3. f 4. e 5. c 6. a; 1. elaborate 2. authority 3. relieved 4. sacred 5. scouted 6. drastic

Questions: 1. Both April and Melanie worry about how April will adjust to school. While April is worried about facing the new class, Melanie is worried about how the class will react to April and her "Hollywood act." 2. The girls had just read about Nefertiti and admired a picture of her head. When they saw a sculpted bust of her in the weed-strewn yard, the coincidence seemed magical. 3. Set starts out as a character in a game, but he seems to grow and develop on his own, with his wickedness running to such contemporary evils as atomic ray guns. 4. The Professor is the spy.

Eyelashes and Ceremony, Neferbeth, Prisoners of Fear

Vocabulary: 1. d 2. e 3. b 4. f 5. a 6. c; 1. resemblance 2. maintained 3. rites 4. exasperated 5. persistent 6. vault

Questions: 1. Melanie takes the false eyelashes home with her on the day before school begins and does not return them until the first few days of school are over. 2. Melanie does not worry about the "February" nickname because it is one of acceptance: it is not a derogatory nickname. 3. Melanie and April keep records of the rituals and ceremonies that they compose because it makes their game seem more important and helps them remember the rituals they create. 4. Elizabeth is a nine-year-old girl who moves into the Casa Rosada. April emphathizes with her being new, but initially does not want her to join the Egypt Game because she thinks it will spoil her friendship with Melanie. 5. Melanie and April call Elizabeth "Neferbeth" and include her in the Egypt Game when they realize that she bears a striking resemblance to Nefertiti. 6. A neigborhood girl is killed. As a result, nobody is allowed to play outside, and the game is nearly ruined. Rather than playing, the "Egyptians" spend the time making things for later use. 7. Suspicion falls on the Professor because no one in the neighborhood knows him well, and myth and rumor have grown up around him. The three girls don't believe the professor is guilty because they do not want their game to end.

Summoned by the Mighty Ones, The Return to Egypt, Egypt Invaded

Vocabulary: 1. demonstration 2. chaperoned 3. teetering 4. summoned 5. omen 6. quavered

Questions: 1. The Egypt gang sneaks away from a chaperoned Trick-or-Treat group on Halloween night. They are at risk if the Professor is guilty or if the killer is someone who lives in the neighborhood. 2. April tells Elizabeth that they have been summoned by Set and Isis. Before Melanie has a chance to express her doubts, she gets caught up in April's pretending. 3. Having become separated from the trick-or-treaters, Melanie interprets a shooting star as the sign they have been expecting. The gods require a sacrifice as atonement for the group's absence. 4. Each member of the group suggests a different sacrifice. The group ultimately follows Melanie's suggestion and conducts a ceremony in which each Egyptian offers up a few human hairs and fingernails. 5. The ceremony is interrupted by an unknown invader.

Elizabethan Diplomacy, Moods and Maybes, Hieroglyphics, The Ceremony for the Dead

Vocabulary: Across — 2. faltered 4. procession 6. clenched 8. bier 10. deciphered 11. mugged; Down – 1. fluent 3. warily 5. contemplated 7. rendezvous 9. cringed

Questions: 1. The title refers to Elizabeth's invitation to the invaders to join the gang in order to ensure their silence. 2. April is upset to learn that there is no room for her in her mother's new life with Nick. For the first time, April allows herself to show her emotions and accept some signs of physical affection as consolation from her grandmother. This suggests that April is growing fond of her grandmother. 3. The meeting of the enlarged Egypt gang goes well. Toby is enthusiastic and Ken is respectful. 4. At first April objects to Toby's taking over. Then April agrees with Toby that they can each choose coded names and send secret messages to one another in school. 5. Ken and Toby hear that their friends are going to spy on them to find out where they go after school. An after-school job would seem boring to their friends and they would cease their investigation. Ken and Toby's concern about discovery suggest their deep commitment to the Egypt Game. 6. The Ceremony for the Dead is important to the Egypt gang because it is the first ceremony in which the expanded gang takes part, and it goes very well. 7. While Toby is disdainful (a "cool-cat sophisticate") in school, in Egypt he becomes an Egyptian and plays the game enthusiastically and dramatically.

The Oracle of Thoth, The Oracle Speaks, Where is Security?

Vocabulary: 1. a 2. b 3. d 4. b 5. c 6. b

Questions: 1. The Egypt gang prefers Toby's version because it is exciting, requiring that they build an altar to Thoth and have the suspense of waiting overnight for an answer to their question. 2. Everyone feels uneasy because the oracle has answered the question and no one will admit to writing the answer. 3. The children are concentrating so hard on the mystery of the answers to their questions that they are startled by the loud noise and even fear that it may be Thoth. 4. The Egyptians consider quitting the game when April receives an answer to her question. At this point, something supernatural seems to be happening. 5. Marshall refuses to quit because he wants to ask the oracle about his lost Security.

Confession and Confusion, Fear Strikes, The Hero

Vocabulary: 1. conscience 2. incredulous 3. theories 4. rasped 5. alibi 6. tension

Questions: 1. Toby confesses to April and Melanie that he was the oracle because he wants their help in figuring out how to answer Marshall's question about Security. 2. The three decide that April, as priestess, will tell Marshall that Security has gone on a trip to visit relatives in Los Angeles. As she is about to pretend to read the answer, she finds a written response. 3. The two return to Egypt at night to retrieve April's math book. 4. The Professor and Marshall save April; Marshall directs the flashlight at the Professor, the Professor breaks the glass in his window and calls for help. 5. April is scared and learns to accept her grandmother's comfort; Marshall is treated as a hero and learns to leave Security behind; and the Professor is no longer suspected of criminal acts when Marshall stands up for him.

Gains and Losses, Christmas Keys

Vocabulary: 1. lair 2. benefited 3. reactions 4. intriguing 5. conceived

Questions: 1. Business improves after the Professor is cleared of suspicion of guilt. The people of the neighborhood are ashamed of having suspected and mistreated him. 2. April refuses the invitation from her mother because she realizes that her home is not with her mother, but with her grandmother at the Casa Rosada. 3. After his wife died, the Professor stopped caring about life and cut off contact with others. 4. The Professor had decided to play oracle to let Marshall know where he had put Security without directly contacting him. 5. The Professor gives each child a key to the storage yard; the children have renewed the Professor's contact with people and have given him new interest in life.